Dedicated
To Gram

Published by
Tallahatchie Tales

Jelly Fries A Fish For Dinner ©

2021 By Jennifer Hill Booker and Erin Hill Williams

All Rights Reserved

ISBN: 978-1-7367380-1-6

Library of Congress Number: 2021902304

Cover Illustration and Formatting: J'Aaron Merchant - @jaaronmerchant

First Printing Edition 2021

JELLY FRIES A FISH

FOR DINNER

Jennifer Hill Booker & Erin Hill Williams

illustrations by J'Aaron Merchant

The worm wiggled and jiggled and
jumped right off the hook
and into the water.
"Plop!" went the worm.

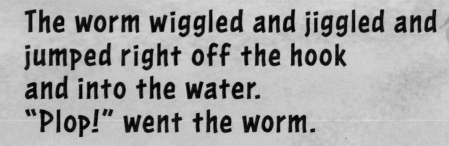

The little girl holding the hook sighed and looked over at her grandmother sitting next to her on the bench.

Her grandmother smiled and told her to try again.
"Practice makes perfect, Jelly," she said.

Jelly was the little girl's nickname. Her full name was Jenelle, but her family called her Jelly. Her mommy said it was because she was so sweet. Her daddy said the same thing.

So Jelly put down the hook that was connected to the fishing line of her fishing pole. She picked up the coffee can at the bottom of the boat and started looking for another worm.

The coffee can was full of worms and dirt that she and her grandmother had dug up out of the garden earlier that day.

Using her fingers, Jelly grabbed another worm, picked up the hook with her other hand, and carefully slipped the wiggly, jiggly worm right on the hook.

COFFEE

"Yes!" she yelled, jumping up and down.
"I did it, Gram! Look! The worm is on my hook!"
"Careful!" her grandmother exclaimed.
"You'll tip us over!"
"Oops," Jelly said, quickly sitting back
down on the bench.

The bench was in the boat she and her
grandmother were fishing from.
Although there were three benches
in the boat, Jelly liked to sit on the
same bench as her grandmother.

She sat there every time they took the boat out on Mitchell Lake, to go fishing. Catching fish for dinner was one of their favorite things to do.

Sometimes her sister Regine went with them, but Jelly liked it best when it was just her and her Gram.

Her grandmother lived in a little house in the Mississippi Delta, in what she called the country. Jelly wasn't exactly sure what living in the country meant, but she thought it meant going outside barefoot, digging up worms, and going fishing on the lake.

After all, that's what she and her sister did every summer when they went to visit their grandmother in the Mississippi Delta.

Now that Jelly had the worm on her hook, she carefully put it back into the water. Down the worm went, deeper, deeper and deeper into the cold, clear water.

Now, all she had to do was wait and hope that a fish would come to eat the worm off her hook. That was the worst part. Waiting.

She had to wait and hope that a fish would see the worm wiggling and jiggling, open its mouth, and swallow the worm on her hook.
Her grandmother called it being patient.

"You're a big girl now, Jelly," she said.
"You'll have to sit patiently and wait
for the fish to bite your hook."

Once a fish swallowed the worm,
she would be able to snag it with
her hook. So, she sat quietly,
being as patient as she could.

Just when she thought she couldn't be patient any longer, her fishing pole jerked! Jelly could see a big fish down in the clear cool water and it had gobbled up the worm and the hook!

"Gram, Gram," Jelly whispered,
"There's a fish on my hook."
"Pull," her grandmother whispered back.
"Pull your fishing line out of the water
as hard as you can."

Jelly did just that. She pulled her fishing line out of the water and the fish too! The fish was on the hook, doing its best to jump off and back into the water. But her Gram was ready. Just as the fish jumped off the hook, heading back into the cool lake water, her grandmother caught it with a big fishing net.

The fish jumped and flipped
inside the net, but couldn't
get out. It was going home
with them to be cooked for
dinner.

Jelly was excited on the drive back to her grandmother's house. This was the first time she had caught a fish all by herself.

As a reward, her grandmother said that she could fry the fish for dinner. She could hardly wait.

She had watched her
grandmother fry fish lots of times.
She had even helped a time or two,
but this was the first time Jelly
would cook it all by herself.

"Do you remember what to do?"
asked her grandmother.
"Yes, ma'am," she replied.

"First you clean the fish, then you remove all the scales. "After that, you heat the oil in the big black pot," Jelly said.

Her grandmother smiled and patted her on the head. "That's right," she said. "Let's get started."

So, while Jelly cleaned the fish and scraped off all of its scales, her Gram put heaping spoonfuls of creamy white lard into the pot.

LARD

The lard would melt and get so hot
that when the fish went into the pot,
it would fry up crispy and golden brown.

Next came the sea salt, black pepper, fragrant garlic powder, spicy paprika, and yellow cornmeal.

Jelly mixed them all together in a bowl, took her big fish, and rolled it around in the bowl, making sure that every spot on the fish was covered with the spicy cornmeal.

"Here Gram,"
she said.
"It's ready for the pot."

Because the lard in the black pot was so hot,
her grandmother carefully slid the fish into
the pot.

While the fish was cooking, Jelly helped her grandmother get the big white platter out of the cabinet. The platter had a red and white design all around its edge.

Jelly knew that it was her Gram's special platter and she was very proud to be using it to serve her fish.

"It's ready," her grandmother said.
"Bring me the platter."
Jelly carefully picked up the platter
and took it to the stove just as the
grandmother scooped the fish
out of the pot. She laid it
neatly onto the platter.

"Dinner's ready!" Jelly called.
"Mom, Dad, Papa!" she called.
"Regine, dinner's ready!"

The fish smelled so good
and her grandmother had
made other good things
to eat with it.

There were french fries, coleslaw, pickles, sliced tomatoes, cucumber and onion, and a tall stack of soft, white bread.

Jelly sat the platter in the center of the table. The fish was fried to a golden brown with its tail curled up and crisp.

Her Papa said grace to bless the food and everyone fixed their plates. Jelly piled her plate high with all of the good things to eat, including a big piece of the fish she fried for dinner.

THE END

Deep Fried Mississippi Catfish

Our earliest memories of fried catfish were at our annual family reunion. Every year our family would all meet up with all our relatives in Charleston, Mississippi, to celebrate our Big Mama's birthday. The celebration was kicked off the Friday before Labor Day with a huge fish fry. Big cast iron pots full of bubbling hot lard would be filled with catfish, brim, perch, buffalo, and french fries. We would eat the piping hot fish on slices of white bread with hot pepper sauce and mustard.

Yields 6-8 servings

Ingredients:

5 pounds, 6-ounce skinned catfish, perch, brim or buffalo fillets

1 tablespoon salt + 1 tablespoon fresh ground black pepper

4-5 cups corn meal, finely ground

3 tablespoons salt

2 tablespoons fresh ground black pepper

2 tablespoons garlic powder

2 tablespoons paprika

1 quart lard or vegetable oils

Directions:

Heat lard in a large cast iron pot, over medium-high heat, until hot. (350*-375*F).

While lard is heating, combine the corn meal, salt, pepper, garlic powder and paprika in a very large bowl. Set aside.

Season fish with 1 tablespoon salt and pepper.

Place the seasoned fish in the bowl of seasoned cornmeal mixture; roll to totally coat the fish with cornmeal.

Fry the fish in 2 or 3 batches. Carefully place the fish into a pot of hot lard and cook until the fillets float, about 6-8 minutes. The fish should be totally submerged in the hot lard while frying. If you are frying small whole fish, fry until the fish pulls away from the bone at the thickest point, about 12 minutes.

Remove and drain on a paper towel lined baking pan.

Serve piping hot!

Meet the Authors

We spent every summer in the Mississippi Delta visiting our grandparents and running barefoot on the red dirt roads. Our earliest memories of fried catfish were at our annual family reunion. Every year our family would all meet up with all our relatives in Charleston, Mississippi, to celebrate our Big Mama's birthday. The celebration was kicked off the Friday before Labor Day with a huge fish fry. Big cast iron pots full of bubbling hot lard would be filled with catfish, brim, perch, buffalo, and french fries. We would eat the piping hot fish on slices of white bread with hot pepper sauce and mustard. Now, our children spend their summers creating their own memories of the Mississippi Delta.

Meet the Illustrator

J'Aaron is a native of the U.S. Virgin Islands, but has made her home in Northwest Arkansas. As an illustrator she strives to create magical content for children of diverse backgrounds. Her mission is to provide the youth of today a window into themselves, through inspiration, imagination, and illustration.

CPSIA information can be obtained
at www.ICGtesting.com
Printed in the USA
LVRC090900210721
693289LV00002B/70